Voices for Freedom

Abolitionist Heroes

By Henry
Elliot

HARRIET BEECHER STOWE

The Voice of Humanity in White America

CRABTREE
Publishing Company
www.crabtreebooks.com

Author: Henry Elliot
Editors: Mark Sachner, Lynn Peppas
Publishing plan research and development:
    Sean Charlebois, Reagan Miller
    Crabtree Publishing Company
Proofreader: Ellen Rodger
Editorial director: Kathy Middleton
Photo research: Ruth Owen
Designer: Westgrapix/Tammy West
Production coordinator: Margaret Amy Salter
Production: Kim Richardson
Curriculum adviser: Suzy Gazlay, M.A.
Editorial consultant: James Marten, Ph.D.; Chair, Department of History, Marquette University, Milwaukee, Wisconsin

Front cover (inset), back cover, and title page: Photograph of Harriet Beecher Stowe.
Front cover (bottom): A series of anti-slavery trading cards from the 1800s, by American artist Henry Louis Stephens. Pictures like this were used by abolitionists to convince people that slavery should be stopped.

Written, developed, and produced by Water Buffalo Books

Publisher's note:
All quotations in this book come from original sources and contain the spelling and grammatical inconsistencies of the original text. Some of the quotations may also contain terms that are no longer in use and may be considered inappropriate or offensive. The use of such terms is for the sake of preserving the historical and literary accuracy of the sources and should not be seen as encouraging or endorsing the use of such terms today.

Photographs and reproductions
Blue Heron Dolls: page 49 (top). Corbis: page 7; page 13; page 33 (left); page 52. Courtesy of the Library of Congress: Image 3a13608: page 1; page 3; page 4 (top left); Image 3b01316: page 8; Image 3c03801: page 9; Image 3b52233: page 10; Image 3a09080: page 11 (top); Image 3g04554: page 15 (top); Image 3g02527: page 17 (right); Image 3a13608: page 25 (top left); Image 3g04550: page 26 (top); Image 0683: page 30; Image 0657: page 31; Image 0999: page 32; Image 1184: page 33 (right); Image 2033: page 34; Image 3b35940: page 39; Image 3a13608: page 40 (top left); Image 3b53030: page 41; Image 3b36744: page 45 (right); Image 3a46661: page 46 (left); Image 3a46662: page 46 (right); Image 3a12898: page 47; Image 1185: page 54; Image 1220: page 55 (left); Image 2118: page 55 (right); Image 3a13608: page 58 (top). George Eastman House: page 6; page 21. Getty Images: page 14; Issouf Sanogo: page 18 (bottom); Rischgitz: page 24; page 27; page 29; page 36 (right); page 37; page 38; page 42; Karen Bleier: page 43; page 44; page 45 (left); page 50; page 51 (left); page 51 (right); page 53; page 56; Susan Njanji: page 57 (top); AFP: page 57 (bottom); page 58. Harriet Beecher Stowe Center, Hartford, CT: page 26 (bottom); page 35; page 36 (left); page 48; page 49 (bottom). North Wind Picture Archives: page 4 (bottom); page 5; page 11 (bottom). The Schlesinger Library, Radcliffe Institute, Harvard University: page 22. Shutterstock: page 18 (top); page 19; page 23; pages 40-41 (background). Superstock: page 17 (left); page 20. Wikipedia (public domain): page 15 (bottom); page 16; page 25 (bottom); page 28.

Library and Archives Canada Cataloguing in Publication

Elliot, Henry
    Harriet Beecher Stowe : the voice of humanity in white America / Henry Elliot.

Voices for freedom: abolitionist heros)
Includes index.
ISBN 978-0-7787-4821-2 (bound).--ISBN 978-0-7787-4837-3 (pbk.)

    1. Stowe, Harriet Beecher, 1811-1896--Juvenile literature.
2. Authors, American--19th century--Biography--Juvenile literature.
3. Abolitionists--United States--Biography--Juvenile literature.
4. United States--History--Civil War, 1861-1865--Literature and the war--Juvenile literature. I. Title. II. Series: Voices for freedom: abolitionist heros

PS2956.E45 2009   j813'.3   C2009-903572-3

Library of Congress Cataloging-in-Publication Data

Elliot, Henry.
 Harriet Beecher Stowe : the voice of humanity in white America / Henry Elliot.
    p. cm. -- (Voices for freedom. Abolitionist heros)
 Includes index.
 ISBN 978-0-7787-4837-3 (pbk. : alk. paper) -- ISBN 978-0-7787-4821-2 (reinforced library binding : alk. paper)
 1. Stowe, Harriet Beecher, 1811-1896--Juvenile literature. 2. United States--History--Civil War, 1861-1865--Literature and the war--Juvenile literature. 3. Authors, American--19th century--Biography--Juvenile literature. 4. Abolitionists--United States--Biography--Juvenile literature. I. Title. II. Series.

PS2956.E45 2010
813'.3--dc22
[B]
                                                    2009022853

Crabtree Publishing Company
www.crabtreebooks.com   1-800-387-7650

**Published
in Canada
Crabtree Publishing**
616 Welland Ave.
St. Catharines, Ontario
L2M 5V6

**Published in
the United States
Crabtree Publishing**
PMB16A
350 Fifth Ave., Suite 3308
New York, NY 10118

**Published in the
United Kingdom
Crabtree Publishing**
Maritime House
Basin Road North, Hove
BN41 1WR

**Published
in Australia
Crabtree Publishing**
386 Mt. Alexander Rd.
Ascot Vale (Melbourne)
VIC 3032

Contents

CHAPTER ONE

Riot!

On the night of July 30, 1836, a mob of several hundred men rioted in the streets of Cincinnati, Ohio. What set them on this rampage was their anger toward the town's **abolitionists**, who had dedicated their lives to convincing all Americans that slavery was immoral and that all slaves should be freed. There was no slavery in Ohio, but just across the Ohio River, in Kentucky, the enslavement of Africans and their descendants was legal and common. That July night saw one of many pro-slavery riots that rocked Cincinnati and other cities in the 1830s and 1840s.

Until the 1850s, most citizens in Northern "free" states were either pro-slavery or neutral. Sometimes pro-slavery fervor boiled over into riots, and several abolitionist newspaper offices were burned down or vandalized. Harriet Beecher Stowe witnessed one such riot in 1836 in Cincinnati.

Cotton farming was extremely profitable for Southern plantation owners. These profits were made possible by slave labor. Slaves usually worked from sunup to sundown.

A Night of Terror

In Cincinnati, a man named James Birney had started *The Philanthropist*, an abolitionist newspaper. Many people in Cincinnati depended on doing business with Kentucky slave owners. They bought their cotton to make cotton clothing in Cincinnati factories. They provided slaughterhouse services. The last thing the Cincinnati business community wanted was to see the wealthy slave owners take their business elsewhere. Outraged, the pro-slavery group, which included some of Cincinnati's "leading citizens," stormed *The Philanthropist* offices. They smashed the presses and heaved the broken pieces into the Ohio River. Then they marched with menace from homes of the paper's employees to the homes of the town's abolitionist leaders. At midnight they attacked homes where several of the town's free black families lived. Shots were fired. This time no one was injured, but many were terrorized.

Eyewitness

A 25-year-old newlywed woman, Harriet Beecher Stowe, witnessed this riot. At the time, young Mrs. Stowe did not like slavery, but she wasn't an abolitionist, either. All the slave owners she had met were **genteel**, educated, and Christian. She also believed that slaves were not ready for **emancipation**, that they were childlike and could not fend for themselves. Her own life was filled with family, religion, and work, but as she watched the scenes of this riot unfold, she felt a deep personal unrest. Something was missing from her life. It would be many years before she found it.

Hatty (as she was called) had been living in Cincinnati for four years. Her father, a minister, had moved nine of the 13 members of the family there in 1832.

Young Hatty Beecher Stowe followed the fashion of the times. Young ladies from religious families wore long skirts, petticoats, and several layers of clothing. This is how Hatty looked about the time she was married to Calvin Stowe.

> *It's a matter of taking the side of the weak against the strong, something the best people have always done."* — Harriet Beecher Stowe

The Philanthropist

The Philanthropist was one of dozens of abolitionist newspapers and monthly journals published in the United States from the 1820s through the 1860s. Others included *The Liberator*, published by leading American abolitionist William Lloyd Garrison, and *The North Star*, published by former slave and writer Frederick Douglass.

There was even an abolitionist magazine for children. *The Slave's Friend* featured stories, poetry, and passages from the Bible, all showing the evils of slavery. Each issue was 16 pages and cost one penny.

The Liberator was published continuously from 1831 until 1866. This poem implores white women to identify with the suffering of enslaved mothers.

LADIES' DEPARTMENT.

'Am I not a Woman and a Sister?'

White Lady, happy, proud and free,
Lend awhile thine ear to me ;
Let the Negro Mother's wail
Turn thy pale cheek still more pale.
Can the Negro Mother joy
Over this her captive boy,
Which in bondage and in tears,
For a life of wo she rears ?
Though she bears a Mother's name,
A Mother's rights she may not claim ;
For the white man's will can part,
Her darling from her bursting heart.

From the Genius of Universal Emancipation.
LETTERS ON SLAVERY.—No. III.

At the time, Cincinnati was an exciting city bursting with growth and change. Meat-packing and manufacturing businesses thrived. Prosperity gave rise to theaters, music halls, two colleges, churches, newspapers, restaurants, and hotels. Thirty thousand Americans gladly suffered the long, bone-bruising stage ride through the Appalachian Mountains for this chance to reinvent themselves as citizens of Cincinnati.

Little did anyone suspect how these slavery-abolitionist skirmishes would escalate. Fifteen years after the 1836 riot, Harriet Beecher Stowe would write and publish the most influential anti-slavery novel ever written, *Uncle Tom's Cabin*. Twenty-four years after the riot, the United States would be torn apart by the great Civil War, a war fought, in large part, over the issue of slavery.

This illustration shows the landing of slaves off of a Dutch ship in the English colony of Jamestown, in present-day Virginia, in 1619. That is the year during which the first slaves were brought from Africa to the American colonies. From this small beginning, the number of slaves in the United States quickly grew to 1.2 million in 1810, 2.5 million in 1840, and 4 million in 1860.

Slavery and the Cotton Gin

What brought things to such a pitch?

Slavery played a significant part in the history of the United States. It began in North America with the British colonies and continued after the United States had gained its independence. Likewise, as barbaric as it seems to us today, the practice of owning people dates back to the beginnings of civilization. There are records of slavery in ancient Greece and Rome, in Africa, in Asia, and in the Americas before Columbus. People of most major religions and cultures both kept slaves and were themselves forced into slavery throughout their histories.

With the European settlement of the "New World" in the 1500s and 1600s, the African slave trade became a huge business. It is estimated that 10 million Africans were forced into slavery in the western hemisphere. The overwhelming majority were brought to South America and the West Indies. About 400,000, or 4 percent, were sold to settlers in the British colonies in North America. The first 20 arrived at Jamestown (in today's Virginia) in 1619.

Most slaves were brought to the southern colonies to work on tobacco, rice, indigo, and cotton farms. By the end of the 1700s, just 25 years after the American Revolution, slavery was withering. Slaves were not paid, but even the stingiest slave owner still had to pay for food, clothing, and shelter. The problem was that most farming in the South was not very profitable. Plantation owners couldn't afford to expand the number of slaves they owned.

Two inventions, the cotton gin and the spindle machine, changed everything. The gin cleaned cotton after it was picked. The other spun the fluffy cotton into thread. Suddenly, cotton farming with slave labor was extremely profitable. In addition, the demand for cotton clothes by Northerners and Southerners alike made slave owners very rich. There was no way they would give up slavery without a fight.

By the time Harriet Beecher was born in 1811, there were 700,000 slaves in the Southern states, many of them born into slavery. This was about one-third of the entire Southern U.S. population. There were also about 70,000 free Blacks, mostly in the Northern states, and their numbers were growing quickly.

Invented in 1793 by Eli Whitney, the cotton gin was one of the keystone machines of the Industrial Revolution. It could produce 55 pounds (25 kilograms) of "cleaned" cotton per day. Although the cotton gin made slave-based cotton farming more profitable than ever, Whitney himself made no money from his invention.

A Remarkable Life

Harriet Beecher Stowe's life (June 14, 1811–July 1, 1896) would have been remarkable even if she had never written the number one best-selling novel in all of the 1800s. She lived for 85 years and wrote for 51 of those years. When she died in 1896, a major publishing house released *The Writings of Harriet Beecher Stowe.* It was 16 volumes long. Ms. Stowe remains best known today as the author of *Uncle Tom's Cabin*, an emblem of the American anti-slavery movement. But she was also a daughter, a sister, a wife, and a mother. She grew up in a very large family with a very strong sense of religion. She had a long marriage and gave birth to seven children. She was the most famous and influential member of the Beechers, one of the most famous and influential families in American history. There was also much sadness and much tragedy in her life. This is her story.

George Washington: President, General, Southerner, Slave Owner

George Washington wrote, "there is not a man living who wishes more sincerely than I do to see a plan adopted for the abolition of slavery." He saw the contradiction between slavery and the ideals of the American Revolution. Yet when he died a wealthy man in 1799, George Washington and his wife Martha owned or rented 316 slaves. In his will, Washington arranged to free all of his slaves after Martha died.

George Washington was one of 12 United States presidents who owned slaves. Others included Thomas Jefferson, Andrew Jackson, and Ulysses S. Grant. Between 1789 and 1877, Abraham Lincoln was one of only six presidents who did not own slaves.

CHAPTER TWO

Hatty

Harriet Beecher was born in Connecticut in 1811. The Declaration of Independence, the document that declared that "all men are created equal," was 35 years old. That same year, 400 slaves in New Orleans rebelled. They met a bloody defeat. Sixty-five slaves were killed, and their heads were stuck on poles and displayed around the city.

The Beecher Household

In the year of Harriet's birth, the Beecher household in Litchfield, Connecticut, was home to Lyman and Roxanna and their six children. The Beechers also squeezed in a few boarders, two servants, and frequently, a relative or two. Chickens, a horse, and a few pigs scratched, grazed, and rooted around in the yard.

The "inalienable" rights of "life, liberty, and the pursuit of happiness" that were put forth in the Declaration of Independence (shown above, left) did not apply to slaves. Slaves were sometimes forced to beat their fellow slaves (left), a scenario that is played out in *Uncle Tom's Cabin*.

A Notable Addition to a Notable Family

The Beechers were a remarkable family. Harriet's father, Lyman, and many of her brothers and sisters, especially Henry Ward and Catherine, would become famous for their achievements in the fields of religion, education, abolition, women's rights, and literature. Hatty would have 12 brothers and sisters in all, although two died in childhood. In a large family of such talent and strong personalities, a middle child such as Hatty could easily have gotten lost. Instead, Hatty would grow up to become the most famous Beecher of all and one of the most influential writers in the 1800s.

Little Hatty

On the surface, young Hatty was a typical, well-adjusted child. She was curious, playful, and energetic. At the age of five, she went to an all-girls' school in Litchfield. Right away, it was clear she was a bright and eager student. Hatty loved poetry, storytelling, and reading. One of her favorite childhood books was *The Arabian Nights*. So great was her thirst for reading that when she could not find books filled with wonderful tales, she would curl up in her father's study and read his religious pamphlets. When she was not at classes or reading in a nook, she played with her brothers in the surrounding woods and fished in nearby streams.

As Hatty grew and changed, so did her family. There were more brothers and sisters, her mother's death, and then a stepmother, and still more brothers and sisters. Throughout Hatty's childhood and young adulthood, the person who had the strongest influence on her was her father. After all, Dr. Lyman Beecher was one of the most influential people in all of the United States, so it was no surprise that his personality dominated Beecher family life.

A Strong Spiritual Upbringing

Lyman Beecher was a preacher who held the belief that it is decided before birth whether or not a person is one of the elect who will go to heaven, and nothing a person does in life can change that. His style was **charismatic** and his message was stern. His fiery sermons denounced alcohol, mail delivery on the Sabbath (Sunday), dancing, and other pleasurable activities—even taking steamboat cruises! He also preached about the evils of religions that disagreed with his strict **Puritan** beliefs. He could get members of his congregation into a religious frenzy. People came from hundreds of miles to hear him preach and submit themselves to the power of his evangelical spell. He was a star.

Young Hatty was driven by a desire to please her father. She was expected to excel at school, to help raise her younger siblings, and to live up to Lyman's strict religious standards. As a 12-year-old student, Hatty won a school essay contest, and the award was announced in the presence of her father. Hatty would later write, "It was the proudest moment of my life."

The next year, Hatty enrolled at the Hartford Female Seminary, a school in Hartford, Connecticut, started by her oldest sister Catherine. A year later, when she was just 14, Hatty would be teaching there.

At Catherine's school, Hatty studied philosophy and foreign languages. She made friends with her schoolmates, but she was often restless and

A Beecher family portrait. The Beechers were one of the most influential families in all of America in the 1800s. Father Lyman is in the center of the first row, and Hatty is last on the right.

Thomas K.
Isabella
James
William
Catharine
Lyman
Edward
Mary
Charles
Harriet
Henry Ward

THE BEECHER FAMILY, 1855.

13

unhappy. She was haunted by a nagging feeling that something was missing from her life. In secret, Hatty stayed up late at night and wrote poetry. She did this even after Catherine discovered her poetry and told her that writing poetry was sinful. Hatty became even more rebellious by reading the poetry of others, including the English poet Lord Byron, who was a controversial figure in European literary, political, and social circles.

The British poet Lord Byron was young Hatty's favorite writer. Much later in life she would denounce him for leading a life that she described as "sinful."

Banned in Boston

In 1826, Lyman Beecher reached the high point in his success as a popular and celebrated preacher. He accepted a high-paying position of minister at a prominent Boston church. It paid more than twice what he made in Litchfield. With such a large family to feed, Lyman needed the money. Although he also enjoyed the attention he would get and the influence he would wield from his new **bully pulpit**, not everyone in Boston was a fan, and his Boston years had their share of controversy and ended in scandal. While Lyman often preached fiery sermons against the evils of alcohol, he rented the church basement to a **distiller**. One day, the church exploded into flames when the whiskey in the cellar caught fire. Soon after, Lyman moved the family again, this time to Cincinnati. Some news reports of the day said he was laughed out of Boston.

Abolition and Sin in Cincinnati

In the early 1830s, Cincinnati was a bustling pioneer town of 30,000 people. Getting there meant traveling by

During much of Hatty's life, religious revivals swept the United States. Lyman Beecher and his followers often attended and led outdoor prayer meetings such as this one.

The Second Great Awakening

Lyman Beecher (right) was one of the leaders of a religious movement known as The Second Great Awakening. It included many religious groups, but they shared a few things in common. Preachers used strong emotional appeals to urge people to convert to their denomination. They implored people to change their ways. They urged their members to reform society so it conformed to the teachings of their faith. Sermons often dealt with **temperance**, women's rights, and the abolition of slavery.

stagecoach through a gap in the Appalachian Mountains. Lyman Beecher believed he had a mission to save the soul of the American West. So in 1832, nine of the Beechers packed their possessions, squeezed into a stagecoach, and set out for five weeks of bumps and bounces. Along the way, Lyman led them in singing hymns and strewing religious pamphlets out the stagecoach windows. Hatty was 21 years old.

Once in Cincinnati, Lyman became President of Lane Theological Seminary, and Catherine opened a new school for women. Hatty taught there and she wrote a geography textbook for the students, but she was not happy. She just could not shake that feeling. She knew something else awaited her. She just did not know what.

Hatty sought an outlet in writing. She joined the Semi Colon Club, a group where members met and read their writings to each other. Hatty published several stories, usually getting $50 or more each time (worth $500 today). Her stories were about the New England people and the life she knew before she came to Cincinnati.

As a 21-year old woman, Hatty moved with her family to Cincinnati, Ohio, so father Lyman could run a seminary and bring religion to the West. Nine of the Beechers lived in this modest home. The porch and columns are typical of the architectural style of the period.

300 DOLLARS REWARD!

RUNAWAY from John S. Doak on the 21st inst., two NEGRO MEN; LOGAN 45 years of age, bald-headed, one or more crooked fingers; DAN 21 years old, six feet high. Both black. I will pay ONE HUNDRED DOLLARS for the apprehension and delivery of LOGAN, or to have him confined so that I can get him. I will also pay TWO HUNDRED DOLLARS for the apprehension of DAN, or to have him confined so that I can get him.
JOHN S. DOAKE,
Springfield, Mo., April 24th, 1857,

THE CHRISTMAS WEEK.

Slave owners offered generous rewards for the return of their runaway slaves. Two hundred dollars in the mid-1800s is worth about $4,000 today.

So far, none of her stories were about slavery. Still, the issues of slavery and abolition began to rattle around in Hatty's conscience, in part because in Cincinnati, she got her first up-close look at slavery. Her first impressions were that it wasn't as bad as some people had said. She frequently visited plantations just across the Ohio River in the slave state of Kentucky, and her slave-owning hosts were gracious and friendly. They appeared to treat their slaves well.

Cincinnati was also a first stop on the **Underground Railroad**, a network of secret routes of escape for runaway slaves. Hatty also knew people who helped escaped slaves, and she heard stories of abuse, rape, and the heartbreak of separated families.

To help cope with the cruel conditions of their existence, slaves developed their own entertainments, including dance and music. After emancipation, these would evolve into many of the most popular and widespread forms of American music, such as blues and jazz. Slave owners would use scenes such as this to "prove" that slaves were well-treated and happy.

Slavery and Spirituality Meet Head-on

Many Americans opposed slavery in the 1830s, but not everyone shared the passions and convictions of abolitionists. Even within the abolitionist movement, members differed over whether certain tactics, such as confrontations that might lead to violence, should be used to further the anti-slavery cause. Like many other Americans, Lyman Beecher was not pro-slavery, but also like many Americans, neither was he an abolitionist, and this led to another scandal that eventually drove the family out of Cincinnati.

Lyman Beecher saw slavery as a sin, but he believed that slaves first needed to learn how to fend for themselves and convert to Lyman's religious faith before emancipation. Once free, he argued, former slaves should go to Africa, where they could start new colonies and help spread their faith to native Africans.

The African nation of Liberia (shown circled on map at left) was created by white resettlement societies. Some of these societies believed that freed slaves were best served by "returning" them to Africa. (Since the importation of slaves from Africa was outlawed in 1808, nearly all freed slaves were actually born in the United States.) Others feared that freed slaves might inspire slave revolts in the South or take away jobs from whites in the North. Through most of its history, Liberia has been a troubled nation characterized by corruption and warfare. In this photo (left), international soldiers keep watch over Liberians carrying food from ships during a relief effort in Monrovia, the nation's capital.

The American Colonization Society and Liberia

Beginning in the 1820s, groups such as the American Colonization Society (ACS) formulated plans to send freed American slaves and other free blacks to Africa. There, they would set up settlements, known as "colonies," made up almost entirely of what the ACS referred to as "free people of color of America." Supporters of the ACS included people from a variety of backgrounds and views on slavery. Some supporters, including some African Americans, felt that this migration was the best chance of helping black Americans gain true independence and freedom from an institution— slavery—that had so rooted itself into American life, particularly in the South.

Most of the support for the ACS came from whites who had different reasons for wanting to "colonize" Africa with free African Americans. Some were white Southerners who feared that freed slaves would inspire revolts among other slaves in the South. Some were white Northerners who feared that freed slaves would take jobs from white workers in the North. Some were whites who opposed slavery but were not prepared to accept integration between blacks and whites.

The ACS persuaded some freed slaves to sail to Africa. ACS leaders helped them establish colonies along a small strip of the African west coast. By 1847, about 3,000 freed blacks from America had settled in these colonies. They united the colonies into the independent country of Liberia, and historians call these colonists "Americo-Liberians."

When areas settled by freed blacks from the United States became Liberia, the citizens of that newly independent nation chose a design for their flag that bore obvious similarities to that of the United States. In a sad twist, these citizens, called Americo-Liberians, denied the right to vote to the native Africans of Liberia.

When the Student Anti-Slavery Society at Lane Theological Seminary held abolitionist rallies, Lyman banned the group from the school. He even prohibited slavery discussions on campus. Beecher was strongly criticized for this assault against freedom of speech. Students quit the Lane Seminary in droves, and the school was left with only six students.

Despite this family disgrace, Lyman's beliefs remained a strong influence on Hatty and much of his large following, even as Hatty struggled to balance her father's views with her growing abolitionist sympathies. In 1834, Hatty had her first up-close encounter with the Underground Railroad when she became friendly with John Rankin. Rankin was a minister, committed abolitionist, and "conductor" along the Underground Railroad who offered food and shelter to any slave who could escape across the Ohio River to the free state of Ohio. He would then help the escaped slaves move on to the next refuge farther north. That's how the Underground Railroad worked. Hatty was fascinated and disturbed by Rankin's stories of the slaves who stayed in his home. Many of these stories would come to life 17 years later in the pages of *Uncle Tom's Cabin*.

It took cunning and courage for members of the Underground Railroad (shown here helping a runaway slave) to stay one step ahead of the slave hunters (shown in background). There were many failures and many close calls.

Hatty's husband, Calvin Stowe (1802–1886), was a man of achievement in his own right. He worked as an editor, teacher, and writer. He also was an advocate of state-supported public education for all children.

Overcoming Obstacles

Hatty's progress as a writer met with many obstacles and painful frustrations. A cholera outbreak in 1834 turned nearly everyone living in Cincinnati into either a patient or a nurse. Then her stepmother died in 1835, and Hatty had to step in and run the Beecher's Cincinnati household. In 1836, at the age of 25, Hatty married one of her father's closest and most loyal colleagues, Calvin Stowe, whose first wife had died in the cholera outbreak. Although they stayed together as a loving couple for 50 years, Hatty soon found that she didn't like being a housewife. Calvin had many troubles of his own. He hallucinated, suffered from imaginary diseases, and was often depressed. Just a few months after their wedding, Hatty was pregnant with twins, and Calvin took off for a year in Europe to study school systems. Her father married for a third time.

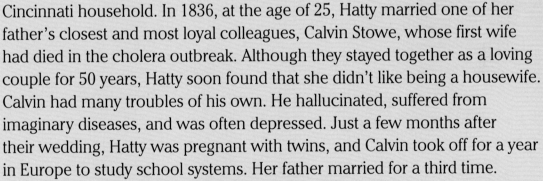

In 1837, things got worse for Hatty and her new family. The United States staggered into a six-year economic depression, and Hatty and Calvin could barely make ends meet. Hatty became pregnant again, and by 1838, she was caring for two toddlers, an infant, and a needy husband. Hatty and Calvin were living in near poverty. She was now doing all the cooking and cleaning and wrote that she hoped she "would grow young again one of these days."

Writing and Other Challenges

Through all this, Hatty put aside three hours a day to write. She managed to write and publish dozens of stories and articles. Hatty needed to keep the flame of her creativity flickering, and the Stowes desperately needed the money she earned.

The challenges did not stop. Just as her children grew old enough that they didn't need constant care, Hatty gave birth again. She had seven children in all—Eliza and Harriet, the twin girls in 1837; Henry in 1838; Frederick in 1839; Georgiana in 1843; Charles, who died in infancy, in 1848; and another Charles in 1850. Charles, Hatty's last child, wrote his mother's biography in 1889.

There was a typhoid epidemic in 1842, and her brother George died when he accidentally shot himself. Another brother, Charles, died in yet another cholera outbreak in 1849. Though she was dedicated to Calvin and her children, her endless family responsibilities robbed her of her dreams of leading her life as a professional, full-time author. Calvin made very little money, and even with the few stories she did publish, the Stowes lived at the poverty line on $600 a year.

It was all too much for Hatty. Early in 1846, she suffered a nervous breakdown and spent 14 months in a sanitarium in Vermont. She returned home in 1847, only to get pregnant again and see her baby die shortly after his birth.

Hatty was constantly torn between her duties as a wife and mother and her desire to be a writer. Her twin girls, Eliza (1836–1912) and Harriet (1836–1908), were the first of seven children for Hatty and Calvin. Eliza was named after Calvin's first wife, who had died.

Cincinnati Pigs

Although Cincinnati was called the "Athens" of the American West, it also had a less attractive side. Hog farmers from the neighboring region would bring their pigs to Cincinnati's slaughterhouses. Before slaughter, the pigs would be allowed to run free in the city streets, eating the town's garbage for their final fattening. This way, people just threw their garbage in the

streets and the pigs served as the garbage collection system. Needless to say, this caused some other problems, not the least of which were the awful smells. Not coincidentally, the city saw outbreaks and epidemics of terrible, deadly diseases, including cholera in 1834, typhoid in 1842, and cholera again in 1849. Hatty was close to many people who died.

Incredibly, through all this adversity, Hatty still managed to write and publish. Equally amazing, almost everything she wrote got published. In 1843, she published her first book, *The Mayflower*, a collection of 15 stories that were all set in New England. It was a success, but maybe even more significant was her 1845 story, "Immediate Emancipation." This was Hatty's first story about slaves and slave owners, and it signaled a new direction in her life as a writer.

Embracing the Abolitionist Cause

Throughout the 1840s, Hatty and several of her brothers, particularly Henry and Edward, gradually broke from their father's views on slavery and joined the camp of the abolitionists.

With a breaking heart, Hatty witnessed slave auctions where a husband was sold to one owner, a wife to another, and the children to a third. She also met more and more runaway slaves, one of whom worked part-time in the Stowes' home. Horrified, she listened to their stories of beatings, rape, and starvation. Hatty became determined to do what she could to assist fugitive slaves in their escape routes through the Underground Railroad. Mostly, though, she felt helpless.

By the age of 39, Hatty had seen her life in Cincinnati, which started out so full of promise, turn into a nightmare of poor health, overwork, tragedy, and political frustration. All that was about to change.

Beecher's Bibles

Hatty's brother Henry Beecher became involved in raising money to purchase rifles and ship them to militant abolitionists in Kansas. To prevent these shipments from being confiscated, he packed them in crates labeled "Bibles." The rifles became known as "Beecher's Bibles."

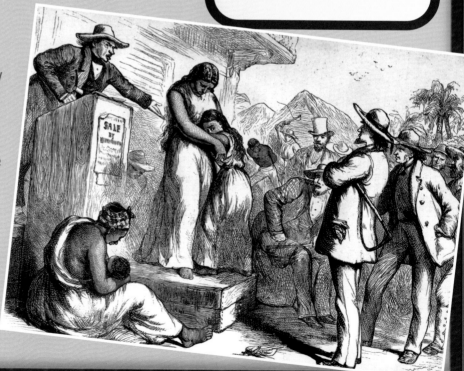

As a mother, Hatty was appalled by how slavery broke up families. She witnessed this happening at slave auctions, and the separation of mother and child became a major theme in *Uncle Tom's Cabin*.

CHAPTER THREE

An Overnight Sensation

1850 was an important year for Hatty. Calvin's teaching job in Cincinnati didn't pay very well, and he got a better offer to teach in Maine, so the family made big plans to move back to New England. At the age of 39, Hatty was pregnant again, and in that same year —1850—the United States Congress passed the Fugitive Slave Law.

Abolitionist Fury

To the outrage of abolitionists everywhere, this law was passed to reinforce legislation originally written more than half a century earlier. That law, which was passed in 1793, allowed federal agents to hunt down anyone accused of being a runaway slave

CAUTION!!

COLORED PEOPLE
OF BOSTON, ONE & ALL,

You are hereby respectfully CAUTIONED and advised, to avoid conversing with the

Watchmen and Police Officers
of Boston,

For since the recent ORDER OF THE MAYOR & ALDERMEN, they are empowered to act as

KIDNAPPERS
AND
Slave Catchers,

And they have already been actually employed in KIDNAPPING, CATCHING, AND KEEPING SLAVES. Therefore, if you value your LIBERTY, and the *Welfare of the Fugitives* among you, *Shun* them in every possible manner, as so many *HOUNDS* on the track of the most unfortunate of your race.

Keep a Sharp Look Out for KIDNAPPERS, and have TOP EYE open.

APRIL 24, 1851.

Abolitionists countered slave hunters and reward posters by posting handbills of their own. Here, Boston abolitionists warn runaway slaves to be on the lookout for "slave catchers" working in the city.

A cornerstone of United States justice is "habeas corpus." It protects people from being arrested and held prisoner without clear evidence. The Fugitive Slave Law threw habeas corpus out the window for African Americans. Any black person, free or runaway, could be assumed guilty, captured, and sent to a Southern state. This print shows a group of four black men—possibly freedmen—ambushed by a posse of six armed whites in a cornfield.

and force him or her back into slavery. Some people who were never slaves in the first place were snatched up without any legal recourse. Families were torn apart. In a direct attack on the Underground Railroad, anyone who helped runaway slaves in any way could be fined or even imprisoned. The law required them to cooperate with the agents in their efforts to track down fugitive slaves.

Hatty could hardly believe that her country's government would pass such legislation—and to do so for the sake of satisfying demands by lawmakers from the South who wanted stronger federal laws making it more difficult to help escaped slaves. By the time she reached Maine, Hatty was a fuming abolitionist.

Both in her youth as a Beecher and in her life with Calvin, Hatty moved many times. She lived throughout New England as well as in the Midwest and the South. Here is the home the Stowes rented in Maine where Harriet wrote *Uncle Tom's Cabin*.

Writing as a Job, Writing as a Weapon

Setting up a new home in Maine was costly. Hatty kept writing—to fill her need to be creative and to earn money to pay the bills, but now for another reason. Hatty vowed to use her skills as a writer to fight slavery. Never before had she felt such a strong and unified focus to her life.

Almost immediately, Hatty wrote and published "The Freeman's Dream"—a story about a farmer who refuses to give food to a runaway slave because of the Fugitive Slave Law. After that, though, she was stumped. She knew it was her mission and spiritual duty to write something

Moving Through More Challenges

Even as Hatty was building up her career as an abolitionist writer, she faced some very basic, everyday challenges. She was a woman with little time to write, no place to write, and sometimes no materials to write with. The six Stowe children needed Hatty's attention, and they often interrupted the special time she tried to put aside for writing. Her father visited and took over her personal writing space so he could work on a book of his sermons. Her brother Henry was a passionate supporter of women's **suffrage**, and her sister Catherine was an equally passionate opponent. When they got into a huge fight, it was Hatty's job to make the peace. Sometimes, Hatty even ran out of writing paper. Still, she remained dedicated to her mission and forged ahead with her writing.

From their childhood until death, Hatty and her younger brother, Henry Ward Beecher (1813–1887), remained extremely close. Henry's love and support helped Hatty get through the most painful times in her life.

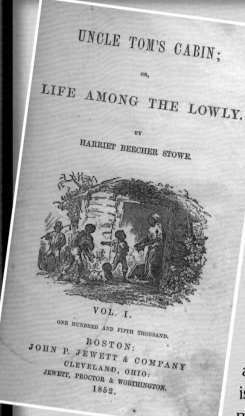

UNCLE TOM'S CABIN;

OR,

LIFE AMONG THE LOWLY.

BY

HARRIET BEECHER STOWE.

VOL. I.

ONE HUNDRED AND FIFTH THOUSAND.

BOSTON:
JOHN P. JEWETT & COMPANY
CLEVELAND, OHIO:
JEWETT, PROCTOR & WORTHINGTON.
1852.

Unlike other abolitionist newspapers, the *National Era* also published poetry, fiction, and literary essays. The best business decision its editor, Gamaliel Bailey, ever made was to publish *Uncle Tom's Cabin* as a serial novel. Circulation soared. Harriet's story was so successful that she soon received an offer from a publisher to print a book edition of her story. This is the "frontispiece" (title page) for the first book edition. Like most novels at the time, *Uncle Tom's Cabin* had a subtitle—in this case, "Life Among the Lowly."

larger and important, but after six months all she had was a crumpled-up pile of false starts. She grew frustrated. Then, in February of 1851, Hatty had a daydream. She imagined an old slave being mercilessly beaten, but he forgave his tormentors and prayed for them. This vision energized Hatty and inspired her to write the story that would become *Uncle Tom's Cabin*.

Originally, Hatty planned to tell her story as a serial novel made up of four episodes. Each episode would be like a short story and published one at a time in a weekly magazine called the *National Era*. The first "installment," as it was called, appeared in the May 1851 issue. Hatty agreed to a $400 fee. That was more than Calvin had earned most years for teaching at the seminary in Cincinnati. Very quickly, though, Hatty realized that her story was expanding. It would have many more characters and many more episodes. The four installments grew to 40, but Hatty's fee did not increase.

Drawing heavily on her experiences with slaves, slave owners, and free blacks in Cincinnati and other parts of Ohio, Hatty drew a vivid, emotional picture of slave life. Hatty also used stories she heard from others in abolitionist circles and information from books written by former slaves.

These books are called "slave narratives," and the best known of them is *Narrative of the Life of Frederick Douglass, an American Slave*,

A Controversial Slave Narrative

One of the better-known and more controversial slave narratives is *Incidents in the Life of a Slave Girl*, by Harriet Jacobs (1813–1897).

Harriet escaped from her owners in 1835. She began writing her narrative in the 1840s, but it took many years before it was published in 1861. Most of the book tells of her struggle to free her two children after she escaped, but details of her sexual abuse were too risky for most publishers at the time. One publisher agreed to print the book if Harriet Beecher Stowe agreed to write an introduction. For reasons unknown, Hatty refused.

The best-known slave narrative is *Narrative of the Life of Frederick Douglass, An American Slave, Written by Himself.* Douglass was a talented writer, orator, publisher, editor, and activist. When he and his mentor, William Lloyd Garrison, broke off and founded two wings of the abolitionist movement, Hatty tried unsuccessfully to bring the two back together.

published in 1845. Hatty was so impressed with Douglass and his book that she often wrote to him to ask his advice about details for *Uncle Tom's Cabin.* Hatty and Frederick would go on to form a close friendship even though they did not always agree on every strategy to achieve the goal they shared—the abolition of slavery.

The Story of *Uncle Tom's Cabin*

Uncle Tom's Cabin became an overnight sensation. Readers could barely wait for the next edition of the *National Era* to come out. Circulation soared, and copies were passed around from reader to reader.

Never before had anyone written a novel whose main character was a black man. Hatty's masterpiece tells the story of Uncle Tom, his wife and children, and Mr. Shelby, his kindly owner. A major subplot follows Eliza, a brave young slave. She and her little boy Harry are also owned by Mr. Shelby. Another slave, George, is Eliza's husband and Harry's father, but they have been torn apart because George belongs to a cruel slave owner named Mr. Harris. George lives and works on a different plantation, and one day he escapes.

Meanwhile, finding himself deep in debt, Mr. Shelby regretfully decides to sell Tom and little Harry to a slave trader. Slave traders buy slaves from one owner and sell them to another. For them, it's all business. They buy low, sell high, and make a profit.

With this sale, Tom will be separated from his family and Harry will be separated from his mother. They may never see each other again. Desperate, Eliza grabs her little boy and makes a daring escape.

Tom and the other characters in *Uncle Tom's Cabin* were depicted in various ways since the story first appeared in 1851. This image of Tom, in which he is bathed in a soft glow even as he toils in the cotton fields, portrays him as a man with a quiet dignity and goodness about him.

An Enduring Symbol of Heroism and Heartache

The image of Eliza, crossing the frozen river and clutching her son, became an emotional symbol of the heroism of runaway slaves. The story line about Eliza, the central image of her home, and the brutal destruction of her family also drove home one of the

The huge green fragment of ice on which she alighted pitched and creaked as her weight came on it, but she staid there not a moment. With wild cries and desperate energy she leaped to another and still another cake; stumbling—leaping— slipping—springing upwards again! Her shoes are gone—her stockings cut from her feet—while blood marked every step; but she saw nothing, felt nothing, till dimly, as in a dream, she saw the Ohio side, and a man helping her up the bank.

— Uncle Tom's Cabin, Chapter VII,
"The Mother's Struggle"

As the popularity of *Uncle Tom's Cabin* soared, artistic representations of the novel's characters appeared in various forms of advertisements and in the popular media of the day.

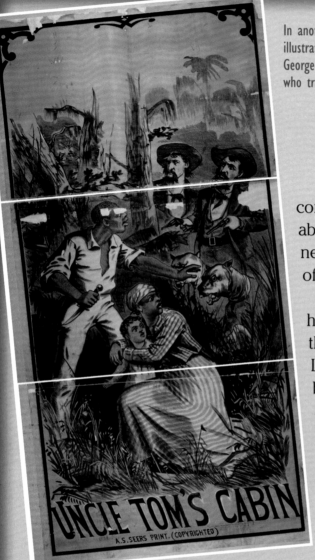

In another advertisement for *Uncle Tom's Cabin*, this illustration depicts the scene where Eliza's husband George is about to mortally wound the slave hunters who track them down on their way to Canada.

UNCLE TOM'S CABIN

A.S. SEERS PRINT. (COPYRIGHTED)

constant criticisms of slavery by abolitionists—that families were never secure from the threat of destruction.

Soon after, Eliza meets up with her husband George. They know that because of the Fugitive Slave Law they are both in danger of being captured and separated again. With the help of people in the Underground Railroad, they head toward safety in Canada. Before they get there, a slave hunter tracks them down. Cornered, George shoots the man. Rather than let him die, they take the wounded hunter to a nearby Quaker village for medical attention. Only then do George, Eliza, and Harry continue their journey to freedom.

Acts of Kindness and Unspeakable Cruelty

As for Tom, the slave trader is taking him by riverboat to a slave auction when Eva, a five-year-old white girl, falls overboard. Tom saves her. Eva's father, Augustine St. Clare, buys Tom and takes him to his family's home in New Orleans. For two years, Tom is well treated. Then little Eva dies of a

Key parts of Uncle Tom's character are his self-sacrifice and love of children. On the left, Tom risks his own life to rescue Little Eva, a white girl, when she falls overboard. On the right, Tom and Eva form a sweet, loving relationship even though Eva's father owns Tom. When Eva and her father die, Tom's suffering and horrible death become sealed.

childhood illness, and soon after her father is murdered. Tom is sold again, this time to the mean and merciless Simon Legree.

Legree forces Cassy, a slave woman, to be his mistress, and he abuses Tom and his other slaves terribly. He whips Tom for reading the Bible, and he beats him more when Tom refuses to whip his fellow slaves. When Cassy runs away and Tom refuses to tell Legree where she has gone, Legree forces other slaves to whip Tom brutally. With his last breath Tom forgives his torturers and prays for them. In the climactic scene, George Shelby, the son of Tom's first owner, arrives at Legree's plantation to buy Tom back. He is too late. Tom has been beaten to death. George is so horrified and moved that he returns to Kentucky to free his slaves and join the cause of abolition.

Tugging on Heartstrings

Every chapter painted vivid pictures with emotional power. Many readers were brought to tears. Here is Hatty's description of Tom after he has been

A. S. SEER'S PRINT. N.Y. (COPYRIGHTED)

Tom's final owner is the merciless Simon Legree, a character whose name has become synonymous with evil. Here the sadistic Legree subjects Tom to a brutal whipping.

sold to Simon Legree: "On the lower part of a small, mean boat, on the Red River, Tom sat—chains on his wrists, chains on his feet, and a weight heavier than chains lay on his heart. All had faded from his sky... all had passed by him, as the trees and banks were now passing, to return no more."

Another passage describes an elderly female slave: "Here, [lies] a worn old Negress, whose thin arms and callous fingers tell of hard toil, waiting to be sold to-morrow, as a cast-off article, for what can be got for her...." In one sentence, Hatty shows the woman's human suffering and condemns the slave owners who see her only as "property" that has lost its value.

Throughout *Uncle Tom's Cabin*, it is Tom, George, Eliza, and other slaves who show charity and forgiveness in their actions. Many readers noticed parallels between Hatty's tale and the story of Christ's dying on behalf of others. Tom's death, though tragic, is not in vain because it makes possible the freedom of so many others.

A Best Seller

Most *National Era* readers were already abolitionists at heart if not in deed. Hatty wanted her story to touch all people, including those who might have been against slavery but were unwilling to take a stand, those who were pro-slavery, and even slave owners. That may have been an unrealistic goal at the time that her book was appearing in weekly installments, but she would soon reach a much larger audience. Before the installments were finished, Hatty received an offer from a Boston publisher to print a book edition of her story. It came out as a two-volume set priced at $1.50. Hatty would get 15 cents for every set sold. The first printing was 5,000 copies. It sold out in two days. In two days Hatty made $750, more money than she and Calvin and the children often lived on for an entire year!

By the end of 1852, just nine months after the first books were printed, 300,000 copies of *Uncle Tom's Cabin* were sold. Hatty's royalties came to $45,000 (more than $1,000,000 in 2010 value) the first year alone. Her book would go on to be the second-best seller of the 1800s. Only the Bible sold more copies.

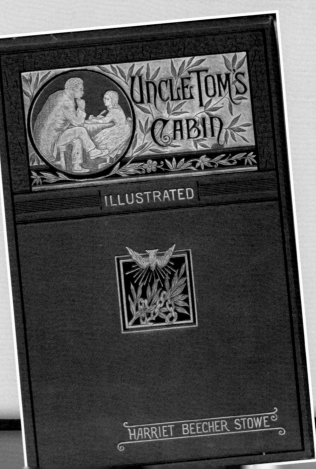

Shown here is an illustrated edition of *Uncle Tom's Cabin* from 1881. Today, a first edition of *Uncle Tom's Cabin* (from 1852) would sell for about $15,000.00.

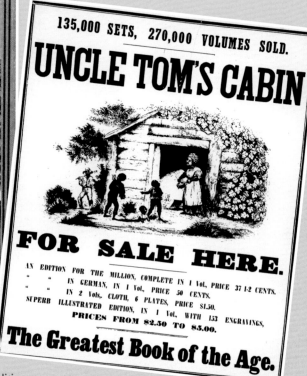

Sales of *Uncle Tom's Cabin* continued well into the 1900s. A "Young Folks" edition was published and it is still available in more than six editions today, including children's editions. Shown here is a colorfully illustrated edition from 1928 and a sales poster for the book.

The Stowes, who had always been nibbling around the edges of poverty, were suddenly wealthy. Hatty, who had always felt overshadowed by the strong personalities of the Beecher family, suddenly eclipsed the fame of Catherine, Henry, and even Lyman. *Uncle Tom's Cabin* sold 1,000,000 copies in England and was translated into 37 languages. Newspapers everywhere wanted an interview with Hatty. Civic and church groups wanted her to give lectures. Abolitionist leaders sought her out. William Lloyd Garrison and Frederick Douglass were frequent guests at her home. She went on lecture tours of England and Europe. Hatty became a figurehead in the fight against slavery, and she sailed that warship with courage and pride.

On the Attack

Not all the attention was positive. There was some hate mail. Several newspapers in slave states attacked her as "a vile wretch" and "a wicked authoress." One person even sent her a slave's ear. One of the more noteworthy reactions was the appearance of what we call "Anti-Tom" novels. There were about 24 of these novels, all of them a form of pro-slavery **propaganda**, published soon after *Uncle Tom's Cabin*. In these novels, all slave owners are portrayed as kind, and slaves are childlike and cannot take care of themselves.

Throughout the 1850s, the abolitionist movement heated up. The year 1856 was an ugly one for the United States. Pro-slavery forces attacked Lawrence, Kansas, destroyed anti-slavery newspapers, and burned down the homes of abolitionists. In a violent counterattack, the militant abolitionist John Brown killed five pro-slavery men. Charles Sumner, an anti-slavery senator from Massachusetts, was beaten by Preston Brooks, a pro-slavery congressman from South Carolina, in the chamber of the U.S. Senate. Compromise or a negotiated end to slavery no longer seemed possible.

Harriet was 41 when she published her first novel. By comparison, Nathaniel Hawthorne published his first novel at age 24, Herman Melville at 27, and Mark Twain at 38. All three were American authors writing in the 1800s.

This illustration shows John Brown leading a group of slaves and other followers in a revolt against pro-slavery men in Kansas, 1856.

John Brown, Anti-Slavery Revolutionary

The same John Brown who led the "Pottawatomie Massacre" against pro-slavery men in Lawrence, Kansas, also led the most famous anti-slavery rebellion of all. In 1859, Brown and a band of 21 men—16 whites and five blacks—attacked Harpers Ferry, Virginia (a slave state), and captured the armory where the local militia stored its weapons. Brown's men took 60 citizens hostage. They expected the town's slave population to join them and start a nationwide slave rebellion. They did not. The local militia counterattacked and were soon joined by troops from the U.S. army led by Colonel Robert E. Lee (who would become a general and leader of the army of the Confederate states in the Civil War). Ten of Brown's men were killed, including his son. The rest were captured, tried with haste, and hanged.

Despised as a traitor by some and glorified as an abolitionist hero by others, Brown was immortalized in the famous song "John Brown's Body":

He captured Harpers Ferry, with his nineteen men so few,
And frightened "Old Virginny" till she trembled thru and thru;
They hung him for a traitor, they themselves the traitor crew.
But his soul is marching on.

Against this background, Hatty wrote a second novel about slavery. Its title was *Dred: A Tale of the Great Dismal Swamp.*

Published in 1856, *Dred* tells two stories. One is of a Southern **belle**, Nina Gordon, and her courtships with all of her suitors. The other plot line tells the story of Dred, a runaway slave. Unlike Uncle Tom, Dred is an African warrior. He lives in the swamp, where he plans a rebellion and strikes fear into the hearts of slave owners.

Dred sold well, but not as well as *Uncle Tom's Cabin*. Then, in 1857, the Stowes suffered another family tragedy. Their son Henry drowned in a swimming accident. With Henry's death, Hatty stepped back from the abolitionist front. Though she continued to write, her next novel, *The Minister's Wooing*, returned to the "parlor" subjects of her pre-*Uncle Tom's Cabin* career. As the fight between abolitionist and pro-slavery forces reached a fever pitch, Hatty took a trip to England and Europe that lasted a full year. When she returned, Abraham Lincoln was running for President, and Hatty was ready to take up the cause once more.

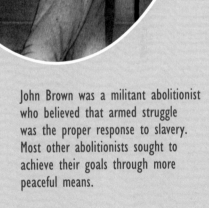

John Brown was a militant abolitionist who believed that armed struggle was the proper response to slavery. Most other abolitionists sought to achieve their goals through more peaceful means.

CHAPTER FOUR

Trials and Triumphs

There is a popular story that around Thanksgiving in 1862, President Abraham Lincoln invited Hatty to the White House. According to this story, when they were introduced Lincoln shook her hand and said, "So you're the little woman who wrote the book that made this great war." It's a wonderful anecdote and a clever, catchy quote, but there are two things wrong with it. One, historians now agree that Lincoln said no such thing. Two, *Uncle Tom's Cabin*, as powerful an impact as it had, did not deliver the blow that started the Civil War. As Southern states seceded from the Union one by one, President Lincoln vowed to keep the United States united. He would force the Confederate states back into the fold even if it took a war to do so. It did. Tragically, that war took 600,000 American lives.

Father Abraham and the Emancipation Proclamation

Even though Lincoln did not run for president as an abolitionist, Hatty and most of her readers saw him as the best hope to abolish slavery in the United States. Although it took a few years, Lincoln did not disappoint them—up to a point. In January 1863, Lincoln signed the Emancipation Proclamation, declaring that "all persons held as slaves within any State or designated part of a State … in rebellion against the United States, shall be then, thenceforward, and forever free…" The object of the proclamation was to free the slaves living in the slave states that had seceded from the Union to form the Confederate States of America.

Many people think that the Emancipation Proclamation ended legal slavery in the United States. It did not. It did not end slavery in states that remained part of the Union. Most strongly affected by this omission were the so-called border states of Kentucky,

After a few initial doubts, Hatty became a strong supporter of President Abraham Lincoln. She believed that Lincoln represented the nation's best hope to end slavery, and he took a major step to that end goal with the Emancipation Proclamation (above). A massive memorial to Lincoln in Washington, D.C., opened in 1922. In 1963, civil rights leader Dr. Martin Luther King, Jr., delivered his great "I Have A Dream" speech to a peaceful gathering of 250,000 from the steps of the Lincoln Memorial.

Missouri, Maryland, and Delaware. Although these were slave states, they had remained in the Union and were not "in rebellion against the United States." The proclamation also did not apply to parts of Tennessee, Virginia, and Louisiana. Portions of these states were already under Union control, and the northwestern counties of Virginia had already seceded from that state and formed the pro-Union state of West Virginia.

President Lincoln had made a careful, calculated move in freeing only the slaves in the states that had left the Union. He felt that as president of the United States and an officer of the government, he did not have the authority to abolish slavery on his own. He did, however, believe that in his role of commander-in-chief of the U.S. armed forces, he had the authority to try to disrupt slavery for military reasons. His reasoning was that slaves worked on Confederate fortifications, freeing up virtually all white men of military age to join the Confederate army.

It would take the 13th amendment to the Constitution in December 1865 to end slavery in all states and territories. So while it is incorrect to say that *Uncle Tom's Cabin* started the Civil War, in a very real sense the "little woman's book" did give a loud voice to the national outcry for the end of slavery.

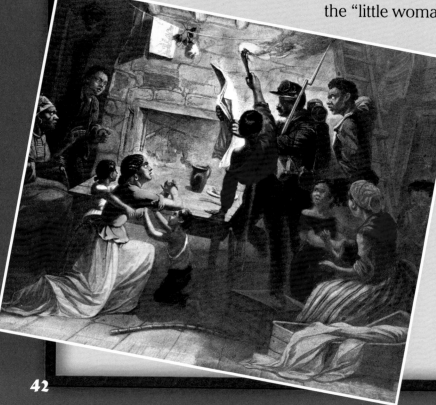

Contrary to popular belief, the Emancipation Proclamation did not free all slaves in the United States. It only freed most slaves in states that had seceded from the Union to form the Confederate States of America. There were many exceptions. All slaves were not freed until the 13th Amendment to the U.S. Constitution was adopted in December 1865, eight months after Lincoln was assassinated. This illustration depicts a Union soldier informing slaves that they are free.

The Emancipation Statue in Washington, D.C., shows President Lincoln freeing Archer Alexander, the last slave captured under the Fugitive Slave Law. Although the statue was commissioned and paid for by African Americans, abolitionist and former slave Frederick Douglass and many people today see it as offensive because of Alexander's crouching pose in relation to the standing Lincoln.

Hatty had some strong disagreements with the "Father Abraham" administration, especially Lincoln's dragging his feet on emancipating the slaves and the half measures of the Emancipation Proclamation. In the end, though, she was a strong supporter of the Union cause. She continued writing, and many of her articles expressed that support.

At Odds with the British, and the Death of Lyman

England abolished slavery in 1832, but the British textile industry and demand for cotton helped support slave-based farming. Later, England sold battleships to the Confederate states. Hatty responded with barbed articles attacking the British government. She appealed directly to the British people to support the Union. Even though Hatty had enjoyed numerous trips to England, both with Calvin and by herself, she now renounced Great Britain and vowed never to visit the country again.

Shortly after the Emancipation Proclamation and Hatty's joy in this partial victory, Lyman Beecher died. He was 85 years old, but for several years before his death his mind had wandered. Edward and Henry Ward had taken over as the patriarchs of the family. With his death, Harriet and others in her family even experimented with other forms of Christianity, something they never would have done openly when Lyman was alive and active.

Easy Come, Easy Go

The publication and sales of *Dred* and *The Minister's Wooing* added to the money Hatty earned from *Uncle Tom's Cabin*. The Stowes remained wealthy. Calvin retired and decided to write a book or two himself. Amazingly, much of this fortune would soon be gone.

In 1862, Hatty began to build an elaborate and ornate home in Connecticut. Hatty was very impressed with many buildings she saw during her trips to Europe. She wanted to include as many architectural details as she could in her home. It proved to be very expensive and impractical. The architectural styles clashed. Some people called the house

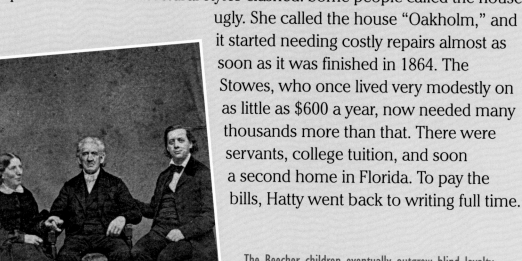

ugly. She called the house "Oakholm," and it started needing costly repairs almost as soon as it was finished in 1864. The Stowes, who once lived very modestly on as little as $600 a year, now needed many thousands more than that. There were servants, college tuition, and soon a second home in Florida. To pay the bills, Hatty went back to writing full time.

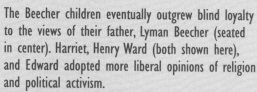

The Beecher children eventually outgrew blind loyalty to the views of their father, Lyman Beecher (seated in center). Harriet, Henry Ward (both shown here), and Edward adopted more liberal opinions of religion and political activism.

The War's Costliest Battle

The battle of Gettysburg was a fierce, three-day battle in July 1863. Historians today see it as a turning point in the Civil War. It is estimated that 50,000 Union and Confederate soldiers were wounded or killed at Gettysburg. Four months later, at the dedication of the battlefield as a cemetery, President Lincoln delivered a two-minute speech. This speech, known simply as Lincoln's Gettysburg Address, would become one of the best-known in American history.

"... we here highly resolve that these dead shall not have died in vain ... that this nation, under God, shall have a new birth of freedom ... and that government of the people ...by the people... for the people ... shall not perish from the earth."

— President Abraham Lincoln

In this painting by Fletcher C. Ransom, Abraham Lincoln delivers his famous Gettysburg Address at the dedication of the Gettysburg National Cemetery in November 1863.

A monument marking the spot where Lincoln delivered his famous Gettysburg Address overlooks the graves of 979 of the great battle's unknown dead.

She wrote about home decorating, child care, religion, patriotism, and many other subjects. A professional writer through and through, Hatty could—and did—write about almost anything. Again, almost everything she wrote was published and earned her some money. Unfortunately, it wasn't enough.

Calvin was no longer bringing in any income, and their twin daughters, Eliza and Hatty, offered little help or even encouragement to their mother. Although they were 27, unmarried, unemployed, and living at home, they showed little interest in helping their mother run the household. Hatty, now 53 and the most famous writer in America during the 1800s, still had to struggle to put aside time for her writing. What created the most serious hole in her pocketbook and, much more important, in her heart, was the tragic life of her son Frederick.

The success of *Uncle Tom's Cabin* and other novels brought great wealth to the Stowes. They were able to maintain several homes, including a summer getaway cottage in Florida (left). By then, Hatty was a celebrity, and her peace in Florida was often disturbed by tourists who came to spot her and Calvin on their porch. At their house in Hartford, Connecticut (right), one of her neighbors was the novelist Mark Twain.

Addictions and Tragedy

When Frederick joined the Union army, Hatty could not have been more proud. Her pride turned to fear when she learned that Frederick was one of the many wounded in the Battle of Gettysburg.

Because of his injuries, Frederick was discharged from the army. When he returned to civilian life, Frederick had a drinking problem. This was a sharp blow to a family rooted in the tradition of temperance.

Hatty tried everything she could to help Frederick overcome his alcoholism. Following the war, she purchased a plantation with 1,000 acres (405 hectares) of land in Florida. It cost $10,000. She hired 100 former slaves and put Frederick in charge. When Frederick could not stop drinking, the plantation was soon in ruins and most of the investment was lost.

During her many, heartbreaking visits to see Frederick on the plantation, Hatty fell in love with Florida. She purchased land and a home where she and Calvin spent most of their winters. Later, at their own expense, they built a school and a church for former slaves in Florida.

To save Frederick, the next plan was to buy passage on a ship that would sail to

Hatty's public image was that of a famous writer who worked constantly at her craft. Actually, she continued to have precious little time to write, a challenge she worked to overcome her entire life.

Chile, where he could start a new life. Records show that Frederick never got off the ship in Chile. Instead he sailed all the way back to San Francisco. Frederick was 30 years old. He was never heard from again.

Calvin and Hatty refused to believe he had died. They lived the rest of their lives hoping they would see dear Frederick again.

The Stowes' daughter Georgiana (1843–1890) was Hatty's model for the character of Topsy in *Uncle Tom's Cabin*. Topsy was a young slave child, an example of pure innocence. About the same time as Frederick's disappearance, "Georgie" started using morphine, a strong painkiller. At the time, doctors often gave morphine to women for all kinds of ailments. In Georgie's case, it was for depression after childbirth. Georgie would be addicted for the rest of her life.

More Scandal

From the late 1860s through the 1870s, Hatty's life was filled with writing, controversy, and scandal. Though she lived until 1896, Hatty published her last novel, *Poganuc People*, in 1878.

A More Enlightened View of Alcoholism

The Beecher family and most Americans in the 1800s viewed alcoholism as a moral defect—a sign of something wrong with a person's character. Hatty's experience with Frederick led her to a more compassionate view. In two novels, *My Wife and I* (1871) and *We and Our Neighbors* (1873), Hatty based a character on Frederick. These works are among the earliest examples of writing that treats alcoholism as an illness.

There were 27,000 soldiers wounded at the Battle of Gettysburg, and Hatty's son, Frederick, was one of them. He returned from the war suffering from what today we would call post traumatic stress. He drank alcohol heavily and probably died at around the age of 30.

Topsy Dolls

Dolls based on the character of Topsy in *Uncle Tom's Cabin* became popular in the early 1900s. Today, several manufacturers have brought the doll back as a collectors' item. Sometimes they are called "Topsy Turvy" dolls that are two dolls in one: the black slave girl Topsy on one side, and Little Eva, the white girl whom Tom rescues, on the other.

Enterprising businessmen made money off the popularity of Uncle Tom's Cabin. One "spin-off" was the Topsy (or Topsy-Turvy) doll. It was two dolls in one. One end represented Topsy, a sweet slave child based in part on Hatty's daughter, Georgiana (right). When the doll was turned upside down, it became Little Eva. Variations of this doll are still made today.

Of course, it was *Uncle Tom's Cabin* that made Hatty famous, but *Old Town Folks,* published in 1869, was her personal favorite. The story is set in the early 1800s. It follows the lives of an orphaned brother and sister as they grow up. One of the adult characters is named Miss Asphyxia because she "suffocates" the orphan Tina by forcing her to work and not allowing her to play. In this sense, *Old Town Folks* was both sentimental and satirical, and Hatty was engaging in a form of social criticism.

It was, however, one of her articles, "The True Story of Lady Byron's Life," that set off a firestorm of controversy in 1869. During her trips to Europe, Hatty became good friends with Lady Anne Byron. Lady Anne was the widow of Lord Byron, the English poet Hatty adored in her youth. Lady Anne shared some terrible secrets with Hatty. According to Lady Anne, Lord Byron had a love affair with his own half-sister, and they had a child. There was more. During his marriage to Anne, Byron was nasty and abusive.

When Anne died, she was publicly attacked. Writers claimed that when Anne Byron divorced Lord Byron, he was devastated and driven to his death. Hatty defended her friend's memory. She wrote her article, an exposé of Byron and his abuse of women. Many of Lord Byron's die-hard fans attacked Hatty, and the debate became ugly.

Just when the Byron controversy died down, another public feud rocked her life. In her 1871 novel, *My Wife and I*, Hatty created a character called Audacia Dangereyes. Audacia was not likeable. Many of Hatty's readers could guess that Audacia was based on a controversial writer of the time, Victoria Woodhull. Woodhull had very radical and outspoken views on sex and marriage. When Harriet's brother Henry Ward Beecher condemned Woodhull from his pulpit, Victoria retaliated. She accused Henry, the best-known clergyman of his day, of having an affair with a married woman. As a form of adultery, such an affair was illegal at the time. Henry became the subject of national gossip and went through a sensational six-month trial. Though it ended in a **hung jury** and therefore Henry was not found guilty, Henry and Hatty were deeply wounded by the ordeal. Today, historians still debate Henry's guilt or innocence.

Ready to slow down

Though she never faded from the public view entirely, by 1881, when Hatty was 70, she was ready to retire. She had had her share of controversy. Looking back, she understood how she was both nurtured and smothered by her family. She could easily have been overshadowed by her dominant father, her sister Catherine, or by brothers Henry and Edward.

Lord Byron, one of the famous British "Romantic" poets of the 1800s, had a very controversial life. When Hatty was young, Byron was her favorite poet, and she fell into a swoon of despair when he died. During her tours of England, however, Hatty met and became friends with Byron's wife, Lady Anne Milbank. She shared some dark secrets about Byron's life that caused Hatty to condemn her girlhood hero.

Looking back, some historians today consider Victoria Woodhull a more important American figure than Harriet. As a militant feminist, Woodhull broke "glass ceilings" in the worlds of finance, politics, and publishing. Harriet and Victoria became bitter enemies when Victoria accused Harriet's brother, Henry, of hypocrisy and adultery.

Victoria Woodhull (1838–1927)

Victoria Woodhull's opinions are often called "100 years ahead of her times." As a public speaker and newspaper editor, she expressed shocking views on workers' rights, women's rights, sex education, and other topics concerning love and human sexuality, subjects women rarely discussed in public. As the first female stockbroker, she made a small fortune on Wall Street. In 1872, she became the first woman to run for president of the United States, even though she could not legally vote for herself. At the Equal Rights Party convention, former slave Frederick Douglass was nominated (without his permission) as her running mate for vice president.

She could have sacrificed her need to write for the duties of motherhood and managing the Stowe house. She might have played the role of the mid-1800s woman and kept her opinions on slavery quietly to herself. Somehow, and fortunately for us all, she overcame all these challenges and carried on with her life and her work.

Harriet Beecher Stowe died on July 1, 1896, in Hartford, Connecticut. At her funeral, the black community of Boston placed a wreath on her casket with a card reading, "The Children of Uncle Tom." Two years later, the great African-American poet Paul Laurence Dunbar wrote this in *Century Magazine*:

"She told the story, and the whole world wept
At wrongs and cruel ties and it had not known
But for this fearless woman's voice alone.
She spoke to consciences that long had slept:
Her message, Freedom's clear reveille, swept
From heedless hovel to complacent throne.
Command and prophecy were in the tone,
And from its sheath the sword of justice leapt.
Around two peoples swelled a fiery wave,
But both came forth transfigured from the flame.
Blest be the hand that dread be strong to save,
And blest be she who in our weakness came –
Prophet and priestess! At one stroke she gave
A race to freedom, and herself to fame."

Paul Laurence Dunbar (1872-1906) was the son of escaped slaves and a popular American poet of the late 1800s. He was recruited as a soldier for the Union army by Frederick Douglass, who later called him "the most promising young colored man in America." Until 1897, Dunbar worked as an elevator operator to support his life as a poet. Tragically, he died from alcoholism at the age of 33.

CHAPTER FIVE

Her Truth Marches On

During the 1970s, boxing champion Muhammad Ali often taunted his opponents. "Smokin'" Joe Frazier was Ali's most famous rival. Ali called Frazier "ugly." He called him a "gorilla." What hurt Joe Frazier the most was when Ali called him an "Uncle Tom." Years later, Ali admitted he had never read *Uncle Tom's Cabin*, and he was not sure what Harriet Beecher Stowe's book was about. The same probably could be said of most American students. Without reading even a plot summary, everyone "knew" it was an insult to call a man an "Uncle Tom." How Harriet's Tom came to be transformed from a sympathetic and inspiring character to a racial stereotype is an intriguing story in its own right.

Today, Muhammad Ali enjoys a well-deserved worldwide reputation as an athlete who broke through stereotypes. He was once stripped of his title as world heavyweight champion for standing up for his principles, but the verbal brashness that helped make him a celebrity and won him the admiration of millions often hurt his opponents almost as much as his fists.

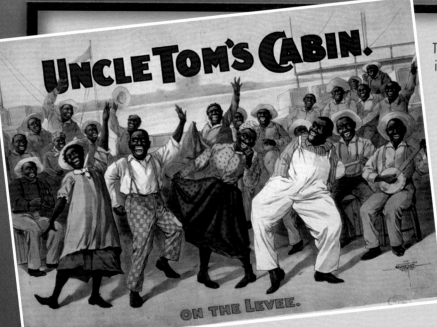

UNCLE TOM'S CABIN.

ON THE LEVEE.

This illustration shows on artist's interpretation of slave life in *Uncle Tom's Cabin*. If this unflattering view was an accurate depiction of Hatty's novel, then it would deserve its current reputation as racist around the edges. Illustrations such as this were done many years after *Uncle Tom's Cabin* was written, and they reflect the racist attitudes of the illustrators, not the more compassionate views of Harriet.

Opening the Door to a Racial Stereotype

First, there are parts of the book that are hard to accept by today's standards. In writing *Uncle Tom's Cabin*, Hatty used many character types that might be considered stereotypes by readers today. There are the kind slave owner and the mean slave owner. There is the obese and motherly "Mammy." There are the happy, dancing slave and the light-skinned sex slave. Hatty drew these characters from her limited view and experience as a white woman in the 1850s. Hatty's characters did not become offensive stereotypes until they were imitated often and badly by writers, directors, and film makers.

Coming to a Theater Near You

Lyman Beecher had taught his children that theater was sinful. Hatty overcame that bias, but she remained suspicious of plays. When offered a chance to coproduce or supervise stage productions of her novel, she said "no." There were dozens of plays based on *Uncle Tom's Cabin*. Even if she had wanted to supervise these productions, there were simply so many of them that Hatty would have had little chance of controlling how they portrayed her characters.

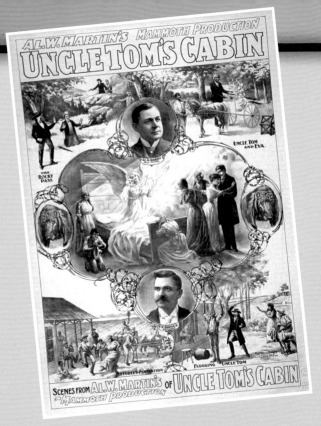

Advertising posters for productions of *Uncle Tom's Cabin*. This was one of the first novels to be adapted for stage and screen. Neither Hatty nor the Harriet Beecher Stowe estate had any say in how these adaptations were produced. Most are only selectively faithful to the novel, and some bear little resemblance at all.

At the time, plays were **melodramatic**, and gestures, costumes, dialogue, and facial expressions were far more exaggerated than in Hatty's writing. Plus, in the "Uncle Tom" plays, the black characters were played by white actors in blackface. The negative stereotypes were glaring. More than 3 million Americans saw one or more of these plays, and that's how many received their impressions of Hatty's novel. The plays were still being performed 50 years after *Uncle Tom's Cabin* was first published. Most of these plays continued what had become a tradition of exaggerated or inaccurate portrayals of the characters.

Then came the movies. Between 1903 and 1927, there were six silent movie versions of *Uncle Tom's Cabin*. In these, too, black actors were

In 1926, seventy-five years after Hatty wrote *Uncle Tom's Cabin,* the last of six movies based on Hatty's book was being filmed. Popular child actor Rosetta Duncan (left) played Topsy. Her sister Vivian played Little Eva. Rosetta was white, so most of her body was covered in black makeup.

assigned to minor roles while the role of Uncle Tom was given to white actors in blackface. Characters' behavior and physical appearances were even more exaggerated. Eyes rolled, and slaves danced right on the auction blocks. The racist reputation that had become associated with Hatty's writing continued to build.

Cartoons based on parts of the novel took the offensive stereotypes to a whole new level and sold them to children as entertainment. These portrayals appeared in Walt Disney's Mickey Mouse, Terrytoon's Mighty Mouse, and Warner Brothers' Bugs Bunny cartoons.

By the 1960s, the long-overdue civil rights movement grew strong. An "Uncle Tom" came to mean a timid African American, someone who was too timid to demand equal rights. In this context, a "Tom" was someone who betrayed his own race. It was a harsh and angry accusation. Harriet Beecher Stowe and *Uncle Tom's Cabin* became wounded in the crossfire.

Today, in the 21st century, Hatty and her books are getting a second look. The racial stereotypes are still being debated, but Hatty is now praised as a writer who broke through barriers for women. Many college teachers now call *Uncle Tom's Cabin* an American "epic," a story of national importance. It is recognized as the book that started the tradition of writing novels with the goal of changing laws and social conditions. *The Jungle* (1904), by Upton Sinclair, changed the horrible working conditions in the

There is no legal slavery in the world today, but in parts of Africa, Asia, and South America, women and children are often taken from their homes and forced into modern and ugly forms of labor, military, and sex slavery. This photo, taken in 2003, shows dozens of slave children riding in the back of a police vehicle after being found in Nigeria, Africa.

meat packing industry. More recently, D. W. St. John's novel *A Terrible Beauty* (2000) exposed substandard teaching conditions in education.

Slavery Today

Today, slavery is officially outlawed in every country. Shockingly, though, slavery is not a thing of the past. According to the Anti-Slavery Society, slavery is widely practiced in South Asia, West Africa, and South America. Women and children are the most common victims. Children are kidnapped and forced to work in factories or fields under terrible conditions for 14 hours a day. They are given little food. People everywhere love chocolate, diamonds, and pretty rugs, but these luxuries sometimes come from slave labor.

A four-year-old boy pounds stones in an exacavation in Benin, Africa, in 2007. The children are taken away from school by their parents to work at excavation sites and pound stones to be sold by their employers or parents for $30 a barrow. This type of enforced labor, known as "bonding," is far more accepted and practiced in some parts of the world than many people realize.

If we do not ask where these treats come from and how they are made, we could be supporting slavery without even knowing.

There are many voices of outrage: Amnesty International, the International Rescue Committee, the Human Rights Education Associates, and the Anti-Slavery Society. These organizations shout the truth about slavery today, but the world is hard of hearing.

Maybe the words and vision of *Uncle Tom's Cabin* will find a new audience among those who are concerned about the conditions under which many of our fellow human beings are forced to live. Maybe the world needs another Harriet Beecher Stowe (right).

Below: In India, children from impoverished backgrounds are sometimes sold into slavery by their parents. They are forced to work in crowded conditions where they make hand-woven rugs that are exported and sold in the United States and Europe. Here, free children in India take part in an anti-slavery protest on June 12, 2008. June 12 is recognized as World Day Against Child Labor.

Chronology

1799 Lyman Beecher and Roxanna Foote marry.

1807 A law is passed by Congress banning the importation of new slaves. Great Britain outlaws slavery and the slave trade.

1811 Harriet Beecher is born, June 14, in Litchfield, Connecticut.

1816 Harriet's mother, Roxanna, dies when Harriet is five.

1824 –1832 Harriet attends and later teaches school at the Hartford Female Seminary run by her elder sister, Catherine E. Beecher.

1826–1832 The Beechers live in Boston.

1832 Lyman Beecher accepts job of president of Lane Theological Seminary. Family moves to Cincinnati.

1834 Harriet publishes her first solo book, *The Mayflower, Sketches of Scenes and Characters among the Descendants of the Puritans*, a collection of 15 stories.

1834–1850 Cincinnati is rocked by a series of pro-slavery riots.

1836 Harriet Beecher marries Calvin Stowe.

1845 *The Life of Frederick Douglass* is published.

1850 The Fugitive Slave Law passes requiring the return of escaped slaves.

1851 *Uncle Tom's Cabin* published as a serial novel.

1853 Harriet and Calvin make three trips to Europe.

1856 *Dred: A Tale of the Great Dismal Swamp*, Stowe's second anti-slavery novel, is published.

1859 Slave rebellion is led by John Brown at Harper's Ferry Virginia. The rebellion fails, and within a month, Brown is hanged.

1859 The last ship to bring slaves to the United States, the *Clothilde*, arrives in Mobile Bay, Alabama.

1859–1878 *The Minister's Wooing* (1859), Stowe's first New England novel, is serialized in the *Atlantic Monthly*, and *The Pearl of Orr's Island* (1862) is serialized in the *Independent*. In the years following, she publishes *Old Town Folks* (1869), *Lady Byron Vindicated* (1870), and *Palmetto-Leaves* (1873). *Poganuc People* (1878), Stowe's last novel, is serialized in the *Christian Union*.

1861 The Civil War begins.

1863 President Abraham Lincoln signs the Emancipation Proclamation on January 1, declaring all slaves in rebel territory not already under Union control to be free. Lyman Beecher dies. Battle of Gettysburg. Harriet's son Frederick is seriously wounded.

1865 The Civil War ends. Lincoln is assassinated. The 13th amendment to the Constitution is ratified, officially abolishing slavery in the United States.

1886 Calvin Stowe dies.

1889 Harriet's son Charles publishes *Life of Harriet Beecher Stowe*, a biography.

1896 Harriet Beecher Stowe dies on July 1.

Glossary

abolitionist Someone who believes that slavery is wrong and who bands with others in efforts to end the practice of slavery. William Lloyd Garrison and Frederick Douglass were two of many abolitionists in 19th century America.

Athens The capital of modern Greece. In ancient Greece, Athens was an important city-state and the center of commerce, politics, writing, philosophy, and drama.

barbaric Cruel, savage, and brutal; characteristic of a culture that exhibits those qualities.

belle A beautiful girl or woman, often associated with a certain group or event.

blackface The makeup used by a non-black performer playing the role of a black person. Such a portrayal is usually marked by exaggerated racial features or behavior and is considered offensive.

bully pulpit A very visible and public position a person uses to express his or her opinions and to influence others. James Birney was a famous editor and publisher of an abolitionist newspaper in the 1800s. He used his position as a bully pulpit to sway readers to oppose slavery.

charismatic Possessing a powerful or attractive personality that can inspire great devotion and loyalty from others.

confiscate To take or seize someone's property, usually by another person who has the authority to do so.

dialogue A conversation between two or more people in a book, play, or movie.

distiller A person or company that produces alcoholic beverages.

emancipation The act of freeing someone from the control of another person. The 13th amendment officially emancipated all slaves in the United States and its territories.

epic A story of major importance to an entire nation. *Uncle Tom's Cabin* has been called an American epic.

epidemic A widespread occurrence of a specific infectious, or contagious, disease at a certain time and within a certain group. The size of that group may be quite small, like a local community, or on a grand scale and extend across a nation or a continent.

evangelical Having to do with a passionate conversion or commitment to Christianity. The Second Great Awakening was a major evangelical movement in the 1800s.

genteel Very refined or polite, especially in a way that calls attention to the fact that one is of a higher social class.

hung jury In a trial, a jury that cannot reach a verdict, or decision, because of serious differences of opinion.

indigo A tropical plant once used to create a dark blue dye, also known as indigo.

melodramatic Featuring exaggerations in the plot and the emotions of the characters in a story. Most of the popular plays in America during the 1800s were melodramas.

patriarch A strong and forceful leader of a family or group. Lyman Beecher was the patriarch of the Beecher extended family.

propaganda Spreading and distorting facts, rumors, and accusations to further one cause or damage another. The "Anti-Tom" novels of the 1850s and 1860s were propaganda writings that defended slavery.

puritan Having a strict code or set of moral beliefs and viewing any variation from this code as a sin. The Beechers moved to Cincinnati in hopes of spreading Puritan religion to the frontier.

secede To withdraw from an organization. Many Southern states seceded from the United States of America to form their own country, the Confederate States of America.

sentimental Full of feeling and soft emotions. Many female writers of the 1800s were dismissed as sentimental novelists.

serial novel A novel published in a newspaper or magazine in installments, usually one installment per week. Uncle's Tom's Cabin was first published as a serial novel before it came out as a book.

suffrage The right to vote. Elizabeth Cady Stanton and Victoria Woodhouse were advocates for women's suffrage in the 1800s.

temperance The practice of not drinking alcoholic beverages. Many church groups preach temperance.

terrorize To use methods that create fear, intimidation, threats, or even bodily harm or death to achieve one's goals.

Underground Railroad A system of secret routes used to help slaves escape from the South to the North and to Canada during the years leading up to the Civil War. The Underground Railroad did not involve travel by train. Rather, escaped slaves and their helpers traveled along a loose network of roadways, trails, and paths connecting houses and other buildings, known as "stations," along the way.

More Information

Books

Douglass, Frederick. *Narrative of the Life of Frederick Douglass, an American Slave, Written by Himself.* W. W. Norton, 1977.

Ford, Carin T. *The Civil War Library* (6 vols.). Enslow Publishers, 2004.

Hedrick, Joan D. *Harriet Beecher Stowe: A Life.* Oxford University Press, 1994.

Stowe, Charles Edward. *Life of Harriet Beecher Stowe.* BiblioBazaar, 2006.

Stowe, Harriet Beecher. *Uncle Tom's Cabin, Young Folks Edition.* IndyPublish, 2005. (www.indypublish.com)

Web Sites

www.anti-slaverysociety.addr.com/toc.htm
Official site of the Anti-Slavery Society. Provides classroom projects, history, and current news stories about slavery.

www.freetheslaves.com/
Videos, books, My Space and Facebook pages dedicated to ending slavery in the world today. Information about religious groups and artists united in the cause against slavery.

www.harrietbeecherstowecenter.org/life/
Official site of the Harriet Beecher Stowe House and Library in Hartford, Connecticut. An excellent resource for information on the Beecher and Stowe families as well as educational programs and a history of *Uncle Tom's Cabin*.

www.hrea.org/index.php?base_id=160
Site of the Human Rights Education Society. Excellent source of study guides and e-classes on slavery and other issues of human rights.

http://education.ucdavis.edu/NEW/STC/lesson/socstud/railroad/contents.htm
Maintained by the University of California, Davis. Offers historical overview of the Underground Railroad. Songs, maps, excerpts from *Uncle Tom's Cabin*, Frederick Douglass, and others.

Index

About the Author

Henry Elliot lives in Pittsburgh. He is active in neighborhood restoration projects, and he spends much time walking along the banks of Pittsburgh's three rivers, the Allegheny, the Monongahela, and the Ohio.

Printed in the USA—BG